The Surrender of Calais by George Colman the Younger

A PLAY, IN THREE ACTS. AS PERFORMED AT THE THEATRE ROYAL, HAYMARKET.

George Colman the Younger was born on 21st October 1762, the son of George Colman the Elder, a noted and successful playwright and translator of Terence and Plautus among others.

Colman was educated at Westminster School before going on to University at Christ Church, Oxford, and then King's College, University of Aberdeen, before finally proceeding to Lincoln's Inn, London to become a student in Law.

In 1782 his first play 'The Female Dramatist' was premiered at his father's Haymarket theatre.

It appears that as early as 1784, Colman had entered into a runaway marriage with an actress, Clara Morris, to whose brother David Morris, he eventually sold his inherited share in the Haymarket theatre.

After her death he wrote many of the leading parts in his plays for Mrs Gibbs (née Logan), whom he was said to have secretly married after the death of his first wife.

His father, George Colman the Elder, was by now in failing health and was obliged to relinquish to his son the management of the Haymarket theatre in 1789, at a yearly salary of £600. Although Colman sought to emulate and build on the success of his father he was not quite of the same caliber.

On the death of his father in 1794, the Haymarket patent was continued to the son; but difficulties arose in his path, he was involved in litigation with Thomas Harris, and was unable to pay the running expenses of the performances at the Haymarket. In dire circumstances Colman was forced to seek sanctuary within the Rules of the King's Bench Prison. Although he would continue to manage the affairs of the theatre he would reside here for several years.

Released at last through the kindness of George IV, who had appointed him exon. of the Yeomen of the Guard, a dignity that Colman soon liquidated to the highest bidder.

In 1824 he was made examiner of plays by the Duke of Montrose, then the Lord Chamberlain. This granting of office caused widespread controversy amongst his peers who were appalled at his severe censorship and illiberal views, especially as his own works were often condemned as indecent. Apparently at times even the words 'heaven' and 'angel' were deemed to be offensive by him.

George Colman the Younger held this office until his death in Brompton, London on 17th October 1836 at the age of 73. He was buried alongside his father in Kensington Church.

Index of Contents

REMARKS by Mrs Inchbald

In this drama are comprised tragedy, comedy, opera, and some degree of farce—yet so happily is the variety blended, that one scene never diminishes the interest of another, but they all combine to produce a most valuable composition.

In the rank of excellence, the tragic parts are to be accounted foremost; and, among these, the original and admirable character of Eustache de St. Pierre stands first.

Other characters, of the author's invention, are likewise so prominent, that Edward, our renowned conqueror of Calais, is made, perhaps, the least interesting, as well as the least amiable, warrior in this whole dramatic field of glory: and yet, such is the equitable, the unbiassed judgment of the vanquished, they profess a just, a noble, an heroic reverence, for the bravery, and other qualities, of their triumphant enemies.

The exception to this general rule of patriotic courage in the French, is most skilfully displayed in one short speech, by a feeble and fearful citizen of the besieged town; in whom extreme terror of the besiegers is so naturally converted into malignant abhorrence, that the man who, in all Calais, is most ready to die for his king and country, is, by the aid of certain political logic from this alarmist, openly accused of disloyalty, because he will not slander, as well as fight, his foe. This speech, with some others, no less founded on the true disposition of lordly man, subdued by the humiliation of fear, would falsely imply—that the play of "The Surrender of Calais" was of a later date than fifteen or sixteen years past, before which period the author must have had much less knowledge of the influence of apprehension in the time of war, than experience, or rather observation, has since had the means to bestow upon him.

It may be said, that Mr. Colman gave the virtues of justice and benignity to the valiant part of the French, merely as instruments to resound the praise of the English.—Whatever were the author's views, the virtues remain the same, and honour the possessors of them, even more than their eulogiums can do honour to the British.

In the first act, the weak, mournful huzza, wrung from the throats of the half-famished soldiers, and that military subordination exhibited between Ribaumont and La Gloire, upon the pronunciation of the word march, are happy stage occurrences, in which the reader's fancy will not perhaps delight, for want of the performer's tones and action.—But there are other scenes so independent of the mimic art, that acting can rarely improve them—Such is the scene in the Hall, the delivery of the keys, the farewell between the father and the son, with others equally impressive. But the highest panegyric that can be pronounced on this play is—that "The Surrender of Calais" is considered, by every critic, as the very best of all the author's numerous and successful productions.

DRAMATIS PERSONÆ

ENGLISH

King Edward the third	Mr. Williamson.
Harcourt	Mr. Bland.
Sir Walter Manny	Mr. Usher.
Arundel	Mr. Powell.
Warwick	Mr. Nigh.
Heralds, Train Bearers, Soldiers, &c.	
Queen	Mrs. Goodall.
Attendants	Mrs. Taylor, Miss Fontenelle, Miss De Camp, Mrs. Powell, &c.

FRENCH

John de Vienne	Mr. Aickin.
Ribaumont	Mr. Palmer.
Officer	Mr. Palmer, jun.
Eustache de St. Pierre	Mr. Bensley.
John D'Aire	Mr. Evatt.
J. Wissant	Mr. Knights.
P. Wissant	Mr. Henderson.
Old Man	Mr. Johnson.
O'Carrol	Mr. Johnstone.
La Gloire	Mr. Bannister, jun.
Workmen	Mr. Parsons. Mr. Burton.
Citizens, Soldiers, Friars, &c.	
Julia	Mrs. Kemble.
Madelon	Mrs. Bland.
Nuns—Mrs. Edwin, Mrs. Powell, Miss De Camp, Miss Fontenelle, &c.	

SCENE: Calais, and its Outskirts

THE SURRENDER OF CALAIS

ACT THE FIRST

A View of Calais, the Sea, and the English Camp

Enter **RIBAUMONT** and **LA GLOIRE**.

RIBAUMONT
Thus far in safety. All is hush. Our subtle air of France quickens not the temperament of the enemy. These phlegmatic English snore out the night, in as gross heaviness as when their senses stagnate in their own native fogs, where stupor lies like lead upon them,—which the muddy rogues call sleep. We have nearly passed the entrenchments;—the day breaks.—La Gloire!

LA GLOIRE
My commander!

RIBAUMONT
Where did you direct our mariners to meet us, with the boat?

LA GLOIRE
Marry, I told them to meet us with the boat at the sea shore.

RIBAUMONT
Vague booby! at what point?

LA GLOIRE
That's the point I was coming to, my lord! and, if a certain jutting out of land, in the shape of a white cliff, with brown furze on its top, like a bushy head of hair over a pale face, stand where it did—

RIBAUMONT
East of the town:—I have mark'd it.

LA GLOIRE
Look you there, now! what I have hunted after, a whole day, to fix upon, hath he noted without labour. Oh, the capacious heads of your great officers!—No wonder they are so careful of them in battle; and thrust forward the pitiful pates of the privates, to be mowed off like a parcel of daisies.—But there lies the spot—and there will the mariners come. We are now within ear-shot; and, when they are there, they will whistle.

RIBAUMONT
And, till they give the signal, here, if there be aught of safety to be picked from danger, is the least dangerous spot to tarry for them. We are here full early.

LA GLOIRE
I would we were not here at all. This same scheme of victualling a town, blockaded by the enemy, is a service for which I have little appetite.

RIBAUMONT
Think, La Gloire, on the distress of our countrymen—the inhabitants perishing with hunger.

LA GLOIRE

Truly, my lord, it doth move the bowels of my compassion. Yet, consider your risk—consider your rank! The gallant Count Ribaumont, flower of chivalry, cream of the French army, and commander of his regiment, turned cook to the corporation of Calais!—carving his way to glory, through stubble-rumped capons, unskinned mutton, raw veal, and vegetables!—and, perhaps, my lord, just before we are able to serve up the meat to the town, in comes a raw-boned Englishman, and runs his spit through your body!

RIBAUMONT

Pr'ythee, no more objections.

LA GLOIRE

Nay, I object not,—I;—but I have served your honour, in and out of the army, babe boy, and man, these five and twenty years, come the next feast of the Virgin; and Heaven forfend I should be out of service, by being out of my master!

RIBAUMONT

Well, well, I know thy zeal.

LA GLOIRE

And yet your English rapier is a marvellous sudden dissolver of attachments. 'Twill sever the closest connexions. 'Twill even whip you, for ever, friend head from his intimate acquaintance, neck and shoulders, before they have time to take leave:—Not that I object;—yet men do not always sleep. The fat centinel, as we passed the outpost, might have waked with his own snoring; and—

RIBAUMONT

Peace! Remember your duty to me; to your country.
Yet, out, alas! I mock myself to name it.
Did not these rugged battlements of Calais;
This tomb, yet safeguard of its citizens,
Which shuts the sword out, and locks hunger in;
(Where many a wretch, pale, gaunt, and famine-shrunk,
Smiles, ghastly, at the slaughter's threat, and dies:)
Did not these walls—like Vulcan's swarthy arms,
Clasping sweet beauty's queen—encircle now,
Within their cold and ponderous embrace,
The fair, yet, ah! I fear, the fickle Julia,
My sluggish zeal would lack the spur to rouse it.

LA GLOIRE

And, of all the spurs in the race of mortality, love is the only true tickler to quicken a man's motions. But to reconcile a mistress by victualling a town!—Well; dark and puzzling is the road to woman's affection; but this is the first time I ever heard of sliding into her heart through her palate; or choking her anger, by stopping her mouth with a meal. An' this pantry fashion of wooing should last, woe to the ill-favoured! Beauty will raise the price of provisions, and poor ugliness soon be starved out of the country.

RIBAUMONT

This enterprise may yet regain her.

Once she was kind; until her father's policy,
Nourish'd in courts, stepp'd in, and check'd her love.
Yet 'twas not love; for true love knows no check:
There is no skill in Cupid's archery,
When duty heals a love-wound.

LA GLOIRE
But, dear my lord! think on the great danger, and little reputation—

RIBAUMONT
No more! mark me, La Gloire! As your officer, I may command you onward: but, in respect to your early attachment, your faithful service, ere you followed me to the army, if your mind misgive you in this undertaking, you have my leave to retreat.

LA GLOIRE [Amazed]
My lord!

RIBAUMONT
I say, you are free to return.

LA GLOIRE
Look ye, my lord! I am son to brave old Eustache de St. Pierre; as tough a citizen as any in all Calais: I was carried into your lordship's father's family (your lordship being then but just born) at six days old; a mere whelp, as a body may say. According to puppy reckoning, my lord, I was with you three days before I could see. I have followed you through life, frisking and trotting after your lordship ever since: and, if you think me, now, mongrel enough to turn tail, and leave my master in a scrape, why, 'twere kinder e'en to hang me up at the next tree, than cut me through the heart with your suspicions.

RIBAUMONT
No, La Gloire,—I—

LA GLOIRE
No, my lord! 'tis fear for you makes me bold to speak. To see you running your head through stone walls for a woman—and a woman who, though she be an angel, has (saving your presence) played you but a scurvy sort of a jade's trick; and—

RIBAUMONT
'Sdeath, villain! how dare your slanderous tongue to—but 'tis plain—'tis for thy own wretched sake thou art thus anxious—drivelling coward!

LA GLOIRE
Coward!—Cow—Diable!—a French soldier, who has the honour to carry arms under his christian majesty, Philip the Sixth, King of France, called coward! Sacre bleu! Have I already served in three campaigns, and been thumped, and bobbed about, by the English, to be called coward at last! Oh, that any but my commander had said it!

RIBAUMONT
Well, well, La Gloire, I may have been hasty: I—

LA GLOIRE [Raising his Voice]

Oh, my lord!—it—'tis no matter. But, haply, you'd like to be convinced of the courage of your company; and if such a thing as raising the enemy's camp can clear a man's character, I can do it as soon as—

RIBAUMONT

'Sdeath, blockhead! we shall be discovered.

LA GLOIRE [Still louder]

Coward! 'Sblood! I'll run into the English entrenchments! I'll go back, and tweak the fat centinel by the nose!—I'll—

RIBAUMONT

Peace! I command you, La Gloire! I command you, as your officer.

LA GLOIRE [Sulkily]

I know my duty to my officer, my lord!

RIBAUMONT

Then move not:—here, sir, on this spot.

[Pointing forward.

LA GLOIRE [Going to the Spot]

Coward!

RIBAUMONT

Speak not, for your life!

LA GLOIRE

Cow—Umph!

RIBAUMONT

Obey!

[**LA GLOIRE** stands motionless and silent.—A low Whistle.

RIBAUMONT

Ha! the signal! the morning breaks:—they arrive in the very nick. Now then, La Gloire, for the enterprize. Why does not the blockhead stir?—Well, well, my good fellow! I have been harsh: but—not yet?—Pshaw! this military enforcement has acted like a spell upon him.—How to dissolve it?—

[A low Whistle.

—Again!—Come, come, La Gloire! I—dull dolt!—I have it:—March!

[**LA GLOIRE** faces to the Left, and marches out after **RIBAUMONT**.

The Place, in the Town of Calais

Enter an **OFFICER**, **SERGEANT**, and **SOLDIERS**.—**CITIZENS** enter severally during the Scene.

OFFICER
Bravely, good fellows! Courage! Why, still there's life in't. Sergeant!

SERGEANT
Your honour!

OFFICER
How do the men bear up? Have they stout hearts still?

SERGEANT
I know not, sir, for their hearts; but I'll warrant them stout stomachs. Hunger is so powerful in them, that I fear me they'll munch their way through the stone walls of the city.

OFFICER
This famine pinches. Poor rogues! Cheer them with hopes, good Sergeant.

SERGEANT
Hope, your honour, is but a meagre mess for a regiment. Hope has almost shrunk them out of their doublets. Hope has made their legs so weary of the lease they had taken of their hose, that all their calves have slunk away from the premises. There isn't a stocking in the whole company that can boast of a tolerable tenant. The privates join in the public complaining; the drummers grow noisy; our poor corporal has no body left; and the trumpeter is blown up with wind.

OFFICER
Do they grow mutinous? Look to them—check their muttering.

SERGEANT
Troth, sir, I do my best:—when they grumble for meat, I make them eat their own words; and give them some solid counsel, well seasoned with the pepper of correction.

OFFICER
Well, well! look to them; keep a strict watch; and march the guards to their several posts.

[Exit **OFFICER**.

SERGEANT
Now must I administer consolation, and give the rogues their daily meal of encouragement.—Hem! Countrymen, fellow soldiers, and Frenchmen!—be of good cheer, for famine is come upon you, and you are all in danger of starving. Is there any thing dearer to a Frenchman than his honour? Isn't honour the greater, the greater the danger? and has any body ever had the honour of being in greater danger than

you?—Rejoice, then, for your peril is extreme! Be merry, for you have a glorious dismal prospect before you; and as pleasing a state of desperation as the noble heart of a soldier could wish! Come! one cheer for the glory of France.—St. Dennis, and our Grand Monarque, King Philip the Sixth!

[**SOLDIERS** huzza very feebly.

Oons! it sounds as hollow as a churchyard. The voice comes through their wizen mouths like wind from the crack of an old wainscot. Away, rogues, to your posts! Bristle up your courage, and wait the event of time! Remember ye are Frenchmen, and bid defiance to famine! Our mistresses are locked up with us in the town; we have frogs in the wells, and snuff at the merchants'. An Englishman, now, would hang himself upon this, which is enough to make a gay Frenchman happy. Allons, camarades!

SONG.—SERGEANT.
My comrades so famish'd and queer,
Hear the drums, how they jollily beat!
They fill our French hearts with good cheer,
Although we have nothing to eat.
Rub a dub.

ALL
Nothing to eat: rub a dub,
Rub a dub—we have nothing to eat.
Then, hark to the merry toned fife!
To hear it 'twill make a man younger:
I tell you, my lads, this is life
For any one dying with hunger.
Toot a too.
Dying with hunger: toot a too,
Toot a too—we are dying with hunger.
The foe to inspire you to beat,
Only list to the trumpet so shrill!
Till the enemy's kill'd we can't eat:
Do the job—you may eat all you kill.
Ran ta tan.
We'll eat all we kill; ran ta tan,
Ran ta tan—we may eat all we kill.

[Exeunt **SOLDIERS**.—**CITIZENS** come forward.

1ST CITIZEN
Bon jour, Monsieur Grenouille?

2ND CITIZEN
Aha! mon voisin! Here's a goodly morning. The sun shines till our blood dances to it like a frisky wench to a tabor.

1ST CITIZEN
Yes, truly; but 'tis a dance without refreshments. We, are in a miserable plight, neighbour.

2ND CITIZEN
Ma foi! miserable indeed! mais le soleil—

1ST CITIZEN
How fare your wife and family, neighbour Grenouille?

2ND CITIZEN
Ah! my pauvre wife and famille; litel to eat now, mon voisin—nothing bye and bye: lucky for me 'tis fine weather. Great many mouths in my house; very litel to put into 'em. But I am French; the sun shines; I am gay.—There is myself, my poor dear wife, half a loaf, seven children, three sprats, a tom cat, and a pipkin of milk. I am hungry; mais il fait beau temps; I dance—my famille starves—I sing—toujours gai— the sun shines—tal lal la! tal lal la!

3RD CITIZEN
Tut, we wo'not bear it. 'Tis our Governor is in fault: this way we are certain to perish.

4TH CITIZEN
Peste! we'll not endure it. Shut up, near eleven months, within the walls.

2ND CITIZEN
In fine weather—no promenade!

3RD CITIZEN
No provisions.—We'll to the Governor, force the keys, and surrender the town. Allons! come along, neighbours, to the Governor!

ALL
Ay, ay—to the Governor. Away!

[Going in a Posse.

[Enter **EUSTACHE de St. PIERRE**, carrying a small Wallet.

EUSTACHE
Why, how now, ho!—nothing but noise and babble!
Whither away so fast? Stand, rogues, and speak!

3RD CITIZEN
Whither away? Marry! we would away from famine: we are for the Governor's, to force the keys of the town.

EUSTACHE
There roar'd the wrathful mouse! You squeaking braggart,
Whom hunger has made vent'rous, who would thrust
Your starveling nose out to the cat's fell gripe,
That watches round the cranny you lie snug in,
Nibble your scraps; be thankful, and keep quiet.

Thou rail on hunger! why, 'twas hunger bore thee;
'Twas hunger rear'd thee; fixing, in thy cradle,
Her meagre stamp upon thy weazel visage;
And, from a child, that half starved face of thine
Has given full meals the lie. When thou dost eat,
Thou dost digest consumption: thou'rt of those kine
Thou wouldst e'en swallow up thy brethren, here,
And still look lean. What! fellow citizens,
Trust you this thing? Can skin and bones mislead you?
If we must suffer, suffer patiently.
Did I e'er grumble, mongrels? What am I?

3RD CITIZEN
You! why, Eustache de St. Pierre you are; one of the sourest old crabs of all the citizens of Calais; and, if
reviling your neighbours be a sign of ill will to one's country, and ill will to one's country a sign of good
will to strangers, why a man might go near to think you are a friend to the English.

EUSTACHE
I honour them.
They are our enemy—a gallant enemy;
A biting, but a blunt, straight-forward foe:
Who, when we weave our subtle webs of state,
And spin fine stratagems to entangle them,
Come to our doors, and pull the work to pieces;
Dispute it fist to fist, and score their arguments
Upon our politic pates. Remember Cressy!—
We've reason to remember it—they thump'd us,
And soundly, there:—'tis but some few months, back;—
There, in the bowels of our land—at Cressy—
They so bechopp'd us with their English logic.
That our French heads ached sorely for it:—thence,
Marching through Picardy, to Calais here,
They have engirded us; fix'd the dull tourniquet
Of war upon our town; constraining, thus,
The life blood of our commerce, with fair France,
Of whom we are a limb; and all this openly:—
And, therefore, as an open foe, who think
And strike in the same breath, I do esteem
Their valour, and their plainness.
I view them with a most respectful hatred.
Much may be learnt from these same Englishmen.

4TH CITIZEN
Ay, pr'ythee, what? Hunger and hard blows seem all we are like to get from them.

EUSTACHE
Courage; which you may have—'twas never tried tho';
Patience, to bear the buffets of the times.

Ye cannot wait till Fortune turns her wheel:
You'll to the Governor's, and get the keys!
And what would your wise worships do with them?
Eat them, mayhap, for ye have ostrich stomachs;
Ye dare not use them otherwise.—Home! home!
And pray for better luck.

[The **CITIZENS** exeunt severally. An **OLD MAN**, alone, remains in the Back of the Scene.

Fie, I am faint
With railing on the cormorants. Three days,
And not break bread—'tis somewhat. There's not one
Among these trencher-scraping knaves, that yet
Has kept a twenty hours' lent;—I know it;
Yet how they crave! I've here, by strong entreaty,
And a round sum, (entreaty's weak without it,)
E'en just enough to make dame Nature wrestle
Another round with famine. Out, provision!

[Takes off his Wallet.

OLD MAN [Coming forward]
O, Heaven!

EUSTACHE
Who bid thee bless the meat?—How now old grey beard!
What cause hast thou—

OLD MAN
I have a daughter—

EUSTACHE
Hungry, I warrant.

OLD MAN
Dying!
The blessing of my age:—I could bear all;—
But for my child;—my dear, dear child!—to lose her
To lose her thus!—to see disease so wear her!—
And when a little nourishment—She's starving!

EUSTACHE
Go on;—no tears;—I hate them.
Old Man. She has had no nourishment these four days.

EUSTACHE [Affected]
Death! and—well?

OLD MAN
I care not for myself;—I should soon go,
In nature's course;—but my poor darling child!
Who fifteen years has been my prop—to see her
Thus wrested from me! then, to hear her bless me;
And see her wasting!—

EUSTACHE
Peace! peace!
I have not ate, old man, since—Pshaw! the wind
Affects my eyes—but yet I—'Sdeath! what ails me?
I have no appetite.—Here, take this trash, and—

[The **OLD MAN** takes the Wallet, falls upon his Knees, and attempts to speak.

Pr'ythee away, old soul;—nay, nay, no thanks;—
Get home, and do not talk—I cannot.—

[Exit **OLD MAN**.

Out on't!
I do belie my manhood; and if misery,
With gentle hand, touches my bosom's key,
I bellow straight, as if my tough old lungs
Were made of organ-pipes.

[Huzza without.

Hey! how sits the wind now?

[Enter **CITIZENS**, crying Huzza! and Succour! **LA GLOIRE**, in the midst of them, loaded with Casks of Provision, &c.

LA GLOIRE
Here, neighbours! here, here I am dropt in among you, like a lump of manna. Here have I, following my master, the noble Count Ribaumont, brought wherewithal to check the grumbling in your gizzards. Here's meat, neighbours, meat!—fine, raw, red meat!—to turn the tide of tears from your eyes, and make your mouths water.

ALL
Huzza!

2ND CITIZEN
Ah! mon Dieu! que je suis gai!—meat and sun too!—tal lal lall la!

LA GLOIRE
Silence! or I'll stop your windpipe with a mutton cutlet.

ALL
Huzza!

EUSTACHE
Peace, ho! I say; can ye be men, and roar thus?
Blush at this clamour! it proclaims you cowards,
And tells what your despair has been. Peace, hen hearts!
Slink home, and eat.

LA GLOIRE
Ods my life! cry you mercy, father; I saw you not;—my honest, hungry neighbours, here, so pressed about me. Marry, I think they are ready to eat me. Stand aside, friends, and patience, till my father has said grace over me. Father, your blessing.

[Kneels.

EUSTACHE
Boy, thou hast acted bravely, and thou follow'st
A noble gentleman. What succour brings he?

LA GLOIRE
A snack! a bare snack, father; no more. We scudded round the point of land, under the coast, unperceived by the enemy's fleet, and freighted with a good three days' provender: but the sea, that seems ruled by the English—marry, I think they'll always be masters of it, for my part—stuck the point of a rock through the bottom of our vessel, almost filled it with water, and, after tugging hard for our lives, we found the provision so spoiled, and pickled, that our larder is reduced to a luncheon. Every man may have a meal, and there's an end;—to-morrow comes famine again.

2ND CITIZEN
N'importe; we are happy to-day; c'est assez pour un François.

LA GLOIRE [Aside, to **EUSTACHE**]
But, father, cheer up! Mum! If, after the distribution, an odd sly barrel of mine—you take me—rammed down with good powdered beef, that will stand the working of half a dozen pair of jaws for a month, should be found in an odd corner of my father's house, why—hum!

EUSTACHE
Base cur! insult me!—But I pardon thee;
Thou dost mean kindly. Know thy father better.
Though these be sorry knaves, I scorn to wrong them
I love my country, boy. Ungraced by fortune,
I dare aspire to the proud name of patriot.
If any bear that title to misuse it,—
Decking their devilships in angel seeming,
To glut their own particular appetites;—
If any, 'midst a people's misery,
Feed fat, by filching from the public good,
Which they profess is nearest to their hearts;

The curses of their country; or, what's sharper,
The curse of guilty conscience follow them!
The suffering's general; general be the benefit.
We'll share alike. You'll find me, boy, at home.

[Exit.

LA GLOIRE
There he goes! full of sour goodness, like a fine lemon. He's as trusty a crusty citizen, and as goodnatured an ill tempered old fellow, as any in France: and, though I say it, that shouldn't say it—I am his son.—But, now, neighbours, for provision.

3RD CITIZEN
Ay, marry! we would fain fall to.

LA GLOIRE
I doubt it not, good hungry neighbours: you'll all remember me for this succour, I warrant.

ALL
Toujours; always.

LA GLOIRE
See now what it is to bind one's country to one, by doing it a service. Good souls, they are running over with gratitude—

[Walks about, **CITIZENS** following]

—I could cluck them all round the town after my tail, like an old hen with a brood of chickens. Now will I be carried in triumph to my father's: and ye may e'en set about it now—

[**TWO STOUT CITIZENS** take **LA GLOIRE** on their Shoulders.

—now, while the provisions are sharing at the Governor's house.

[**CITIZENS** let him fall.

ALL
Sharing provisions! Allons! vite!—away! away!

[Exeunt **CITIZENS** hastily.

LA GLOIRE
Oh diable! this is popularity. Adieu, my grateful neighbours! Thus does many a fool-hardy booby, like me, run his head into danger; and a few empty huzzas, which leave him at the next turning of a corner, are all he gets for his pains. Now, while all the town is gone to dinner, will I go to woo. My poor Madelon must be woefully fallen away, since I quitted Calais, Heigho! I've lost, I warrant me, a good half of my mistress since we parted. I have secured for her the daintiest bits of our whole cargo, as marks of my affection. A butcher couldn't show her more tenderness than I shall. If love were now weighed out by

the pound, bating my master, the Count Ribaumont, who is in love with Lady Julia, not all the men in the city could balance the scales with me.

[Exit.

SCENE III

A Hall, in the House of John de Vienne

Enter **JULIA** and **O'CARROL**.

JULIA
Now, O'Carrol; what is the time of day?

O'CARROL
Fait, Lady Julia, we might have called it a little past breakfast time, formerly; but since the fashion of eating has been worn out in Calais, a man may be content to say it bears hard upon ten. Och! if clocks were jacks now, time would stand still; and the year would go down, for the want of winding up every now and then.

JULIA
Saw you my father this morning?

O'CARROL
You may say that.

JULIA
How looked he, O'Carrol?

O'CARROL
By my soul! Lady Julia, that old father of yours, and master of mine, is a gallant gentleman. And gallantly he bears himself. For certain, and so he ought; being a Knight of Burgundy, and Governor of Calais; but if I was Governor just now, to be sure I should not like to take a small trip from Calais, one morning, just to see what sort of a knight I was in Burgundy.

JULIA
Who has he in his company?

O'CARROL
Why, madam, why—now dare not I tell who, for fear of offending her.—Company? Why, to be sure I have been in his company:—for want of finer acquaintance, madam, he was e'en forced to put up, half an hour, with an humble friend.

JULIA
Poor fool! thy words are shrewder than thy meaning.
How many crowd the narrow space of life

With those gay, gaudy flowers of society,
Those annuals, call'd acquaintance; which do fade
And die away, ere we can say they blosom;
Mocking the idle cultivator's care,
From year to year; while one poor slip of friendship,
Hardy, tho' modest, stands the winter's frost,
And cheers its owner's eye with evergreen!

O'CARROL
Troth, lady, one honest potatoe in a garden is worth an hundred beds of your good-for-nothing tulips. Oh! 'tis meat and drink to me to see a friend! and, truly 'tis lucky, in this time of famine, to have one in the house to look at, to keep me from starving. Little did I think, eight years ago, when I came over among fifty thousand brave boys—English, Irish, and else,—to fight under King Edward, who now lies before Calais here, that I should find such a warm soul towards me in a Frenchman's body;—especially when the business, that brought me, was to help to give his countrymen a beating.

JULIA
Thy gratitude, O'Carrol, has well repaid the pains my father took in preserving thee.

O'CARROL
Gratitude! fait, madam, begging your pardon, 'tis no such thing; 'tis nothing but showing the sense I have of my obligation. There was I, in the year 1339, in the English camp—on the fields of Vianfosse, near Capelle—which never came to an action; excepting a trifling bit of skirmish, in which my good cruel friends left me for dead out of our lines; when a kind enemy—your father—(a blessing on his friendly heart for it!) picked me up, and set the breath agoing again, that was almost thumped out of my body. He saved my life; it is but a poor commodity;—but, as long as it lasts, by my soul! he and his family shall have the wear and tear of it.

JULIA
Thou hast been a trusty follower, O'Carrol; nay, more a friend than follower; thou art entwined in all the interests of our house, and art as attached to me as to my father.

O'CARROL
Ay, troth, Lady Julia, and a good deal more; more shame to me for it; because I am indebted for all to the Governor. I don't know how it may be with wiser nations, but if regard is to go to a whole family, there's a something about the female part of it that an Irishman can't help giving the preference to, for the soul of him.

JULIA
But, tell me, who is with my father?

O'CARROL
Indeed that I will not—for a reason.

JULIA
And what may the reason be?

O'CARROL

Because, long before he arrived, you bid me never mention his name. It may be, perhaps, the noble gentleman who has just succoured the town.—Well, if I must not say who is with my master, I may say who my master is with.—It is the Count Ribaumont.

JULIA
Why should I tremble at that name? Why should my tongue be now constrained to speak the language of my heart? O father! father!

O'CARROL
Och—ho!

JULIA
Why dost thou sigh, O'Carrol?

O'CARROL
Truly, madam, I was thinking of a piece of a rich old uncle I had in Ireland; who sent me to the French wars, to tear me away from a dear little creature I loved better than my eyes.

JULIA
And wast thou ever in love, O'Carrol?

O'CARROL
That I was, faith, up to my chin. I never think upon it but it remembers me of the song that was wont to be played by honest Clamoran, poor fellow, our minstrel, in the north.

JULIA
I pr'ythee sing it to me, good O'Carrol;
For there is something in these artless ditties,
Expressive of a simple soul in love,
That fills the mind with pleasing melancholy.

SONG.—O'CARROL.
Oh! the moment was sad when my love and I parted;
Savourna deligh shighan ogh!
As I kiss'd off her tears, I was nigh broken hearted;
Savourna deligh shighan ogh;
Wan was her cheek, which hung on my shoulder;
Damp was her hand, no marble was colder;
I felt that I never again should behold her.
Savourna deligh shighan ogh!
Long I fought for my country, far, far from my true love;
Savourna deligh shighan ogh!
All my pay and my booty I hoarded for you, love;
Savourna deligh shighan ogh!
Peace was proclaim'd,—escaped from the slaughter,
Landed at home—my sweet girl I sought her;
But sorrow, alas! to the cold grave had brought her.
Savourna deligh shighan ogh!

[Enter **JOHN de VIENNE** and **RIBAUMONT**.

JOHN de VIENNE
Nay, nay, my lord! you're welcome.
Yet, were I private here, some prudent qualms,
Which you well wot, I trow, my noble lord!
Might cause me flatly sound that full toned welcome,
Which breathes the mellow note of hospitality.
Yet, being Governor of Calais here—
But take me with you, Count,—I can discern
Your noble virtues; ay, and love them too;
Did not a father's care—but let that pass.—
Julia, my girl—the Count of Ribaumont:—
Thank the brave champion of our city.

JULIA
Sir!
Tho' one poor simple drop of gratitude,
Amid the boisterous tide of general thanks,
Can little swell the glory of your enterprise,
Accept it freely.—You are welcome, sir.

RIBAUMONT
Cold does it seem to me.—'Sdeath! this is ice!
Freezing indifference:—down, down, my heart!

[Aside.

I pray you, lady, do not strain your courtesy.
If I have reap'd a single grain of favour,
From your fair self, and noble father here,
I have obtain'd the harvest of my hope.

JOHN de VIENNE
Heyday! here's bow, and jut, and cringe, and scrape!—
Count! I have served in battle; witness for me
Some curious scars, the soldier's coxcombry,
In which he struts, fantastically carved
Upon the tough old doublet nature gave him.
Let us, then, speak like brothers of the field;
Roundly and blunt. Have I your leave, my lord?

RIBAUMONT
As freely, sir, as you have ask'd it.

JOHN de VIENNE
Thus, then:

I have a daughter, look you; here she stands;
Right fair and virtuous;—

[**COUNT** attempts to speak.

Nay, Count, spare your speech;
I know I've your assent to the position:
I have a king too; and from whom 'tis signified
My daughter must be match'd with (speedily)
A certain lord about the royal person.—
Now, tho' there may be some, whose gallant bearing
(And glean from this, Count, what it is I aim at,)
I might be proud to be allied to, yet
Being a veteran French soldier, stuff'd
With right enthusiastic loyalty,
My house, myself, my child—Heaven knows I love her!—
Should perish, piece-meal, ere I could infringe
The faintest line or trace of the proceeding,
The king, our master, honours me in marking.

RIBAUMONT
I do conceive you, sir.

JOHN de VIENNE
Why, then, conceiving,
Once more, right welcome, Count. I lodge you here,
As my good friend—and Julia's friend—the friend
To all our city.—Tut, Count, love is boys' play;
A soldier has not time for't.—
Come, Count.—Within there, hoa! we need refreshment,
Which you have furnish'd.—Love? pish! love's a gew-gaw.
Nay, come, Count, come.

[Exit.

JULIA
Sir, will it please you follow?

RIBAUMONT
I fain would speak one word, and—'sdeath! I cannot.—
Pardon me, madam; I attend.—Oh, Julia!

[Exit, leading out **JULIA**.

O'CARROL
Och ho! poor dear creatures, my heart bleeds for them. To be sure the ould gentleman means all for the best, and what he talks must be right: but if love is a gew-gaw, as he says, by my soul! 'tis the prettiest plaything for children, from sixteen to five-and-twenty, that ever was invented!

[Exit.

The English Camp

Enter **KING**, **SIR WALTER MANNY**, **HARCOURT**, **ARUNDEL**, **WARWICK**, and **ATTENDANTS**.

KING
Fie, lords! it slurs our name;—the town is succour'd.
'Twas dull neglect to let them pass: a blot
Upon our English camp; where vigilance
Should be the watch-word. Which way got they in?

SIR WALTER MANNY
By sea, as we do learn, my gracious liege?

KING
Where was our fleet then? does it ride the ocean
In idle mockery? It should float to awe
These Frenchmen here. How are they stored, my lord?

HARCOURT
Barely, as it should seem. Their crazy vessel,
Driven among the rocks, that skirt the shore,
Let in the waves so fast upon the cargo,
The better half is either sunk or spoilt.
They scarce can hold another day, my liege.

KING
Thanks to the sea for't—not our Admiral.
They brave it, stubborn, to the very last:—
But they shall smart for't shortly; smart severely.
Meantime, prepare we for our Queen; who comes
From England, deck'd in conquest. Say, Lord Harcourt,
Are all prepared to welcome her arrival?

HARCOURT
All, my dread liege. The beach is thickly lined
With English soldiery, in ardent watch,
Fixing their eyes upon the bark, which bears
Our royal mistress. It was hoped, ere this,
'T had reach'd the harbour.—

[Grand Flourish.

Hark! the queen has landed.

KING
Do you then, good my lord! escort her hither.

[Exit **HARCOURT**.

Sir Walter Manny?

SIR WALTER MANNY
Ay, my gracious sovereign.

KING
Guard well this packet. When the Governor
Of this same peevish town shall call a parley,
Break you it up, and from it speak our pleasure.
Here are the terms—the only terms—on which
We do allow them to capitulate.

[Enter the **QUEEN PHILIPPA**, attended.

Oh, welcome! welcome! We shall give you here
Rude martial fare, and soldiers' entertainment.

QUEEN PHILIPPA
Royal sir!
Well met, and happily. I learn your labours
Draw to a glorious end.—When you return,
Besides the loyal subjects who would greet you,
The Scottish king, my lord! waits your arrival;
Who, somewhat partial to his neighbour's land,
Did come an uninvited guest among us.
I doubt he'll think us over-hospitable;
For, dreading his too quick departure from us,
I have made bold to guard him in the Tower:
And hither have I sail'd, my noble liege!
To glad you with the tidings.

KING
My sweet warrior!
We will dispatch our work here, then for England.
Calais will soon be ours;—of that hereafter.
Think we, to-day, on nought but revelry.
You, madam, shall diffuse your influence
Throughout our camp.—Strike, there, our martial music!
For want of better, good Philippa, take
A soldier's noisy concert. Strike! I say.

GRAND CHORUS.

War has still its melody;—
When blows come thick, and arrows fly,
When the soldier marches o'er
The crimson field, knee-deep in gore,
By carnage, and grim death, surrounded,
And groans of dying men confounded;—
If the warlike drum he hear,
And the shrill trumpet strike his ear.
Roused by the spirit-stirring tones,
Music's influence he owns;
His lusty heart beats quick, and high;
War has still its melody.
But, when the hard fought day is done,
And the battle's fairly won;
Oh! then he trolls the jolly note,
In triumph, thro' his rusty throat;
And all the story of the strife
He carols to the merry fife.
His comrades join, their feats to tell;
The chorus then begins to swell;
Loud martial music rends the sky:
This is the soldier's melody.

ACT THE SECOND

SCENE I

Madelon's Apartment

LA GLOIRE and **MADELON** discovered. **MADELON** seated at a Table covered with Eatables, Wines, &c. **LA GLOIRE** standing near the Table.

LA GLOIRE

Blessings on her heart, how cleverly she feeds! the meat goes as naturally into her little mouth, as if it had been used to the road all the time of the famine: though, Heaven knows, 'tis a path that has, lately, been little frequented.

MADELON

A votre santé, mon ami;—your health, La Gloire.

[Drinks.

LA GLOIRE

Nay, I'll answer thee in that, though bumpers were Englishmen, and went against my French stomach.

[Takes Wine.

Heaven bless thee, my poor Madelon! May a woman never tumble into the mire of distress; and, if she is in, ill befall him that won't help her clean out again.

[Drinks.

MADELON
There; enough.

[Comes from Table.

LA GLOIRE
So: one kiss for a bonne bouche.—

[Kisses her.

—Dost love me the better for this feast, now, Madelon?

MADELON
No, truly, not a jot. I love you e'en as well before dinner as after.

LA GLOIRE
What a jewel is regular affection!—to love, equally, through the week, maigre days, and all! I cannot but own a full meal makes an improvement in the warmth of my feelings. I can eat and drink myself into a glow of tenderness, that fasting can never come up to. And what hast thou done in my absence, Madelon?

MADELON
Little, La Gloire, but grieve with the rest. I have thought on you; gone to confession in the morning; seemed happy, in the day, to cheer my poor old father:—but my heart was bursting, La Gloire:—and, at night, by myself, I looked at this little cross you gave me, and cried.

LA GLOIRE [Smothering his Tears]
Madelon, I,—I—I want another draught of burgundy.

[Drinks.

MADELON
Once, indeed,—I thought it was hard,—Father Antony enjoined me penance, for thinking so much about you.

LA GLOIRE
An old—What, by putting peas in your shoes, as usual?

MADELON
Yes; but, as it happened, I escaped.

LA GLOIRE

Ay, marry! how?

MADELON

Why, as the famine pressed, the holy fathers had boiled all our punishments, in puddings for the convent; and there was not a penitential pea left in the town.

LA GLOIRE

O, gluttony! to deprive the innocent of their hard, dry penances, and apply them, soft, to their own offending stomachs! I never could abide these pampered friars. They are the pot-bellied children of the Pope, nursed at the bosom of old mother church; and plaguy chubby boys they are. One convent of them, in a town, breeds a famine sooner than an English blockade. But, what says thy father within, here, Madelon, to our marriage?

MADELON

Truly, he has no objection, but in respect to your being a soldier.

LA GLOIRE

Sacre bleu! object to my carrying arms! my glory! my pride!

MADELON

Pr'ythee, now, 'tis not for that.

LA GLOIRE

Degrade my profession!—my—look ye, Madelon; I love thee with all my heart—with an honest soldier's heart—else I could tell your father, that a citizen could never get on in the world, without a soldier to do his journey-work:—and your soldier, look ye—'sblood! it makes me fret like a hot day's march!—your soldier, in all nations, when he is rusted down to your quiet citizen, and so sets up at home for himself, is in double respect, for having served such an honourable apprenticeship.

MADELON

Nay, now, La Gloire, my father meant not—

LA GLOIRE

Marry, I would tell your father this to his teeth; which, were it not for my captain and me—two soldiers, mark you me—might not, haply, have been so soon set a going.

MADELON

Ungenerous! I could not have spoken such cutting words to you, La Gloire.—My poor father only meant, that the wars might separate us. But I had a remedy for that, too, for all your unkindness.

LA GLOIRE

Pish!—remedy?—well—psha!—what was the remedy, Madelon?

MADELON

Why, I could have followed you to the camp.

LA GLOIRE
And wouldst thou follow me then?

MADELON
Ay, surely, La Gloire: I could follow him I love all over the world.

LA GLOIRE
And bear the fatigue of a campaign, Madelon?

MADELON
Any thing with you, **LA GLOIRE**
I warrant us, we should be happy enough. Ay, and I could be useful too. I could pack your knapsack; sing canzonets with you, to make us merry on a day's march; mix in the soldier's dance upon occasion; and, at sun-set, I would dress up our little tent, as neat as any captain's in the field: then, at supper, La Gloire, we should be as cheerful!—

LA GLOIRE
Now could I cut my tongue out for what I have said!—Cuff me; slap my face, Madelon; then kiss me, and forgive me: and, if ever I bestride my great war-horse again, and let him run away with me, and trample over the heart of my best friends, I wish he may kick me off, and break my neck in a ditch for my pains.—But—what—ha! ha!—what should we do with our children, Madelon?

MADELON
Ah! mon Dieu! I had forgot that:—but if your endeavours be honest, La Gloire, Providence will take care of them, I warrant you.

DUET. LA GLOIRE AND MADELON.
MADELON
Could you to battle march away,
And leave me here complaining?
I'm sure 'twould break my heart to stay,
When you are gone campaigning.
Ah! non, non, non!
Pauvre Madelon
Could never quit her rover:
Ah! non, non, non!
Pauvre Madelon
Would go with you all the world over.

LA GLOIRE
No, no, my love! ah! do not grieve;
A soldier true you'll find me:
I could not have the heart to leave
My little girl behind me.
Ah! non, non, non!
Pauvre Madelon
Should never quit her rover:
Ah! non, non, non!

Pauvre Madelon
Should go with me all the world over.

BOTH
Then let the world jog as it will,
Let hollow friends forsake us,
We both shall be as happy still
As war and love can make us.
Ah! non, non, non!
Pauvre Madelon
Shall never quit her rover:
Ah! non, non, non!
Pauvre Madelon
Shall go with {you/me} all the world over.

LA GLOIRE
By the mass, Madelon, such a wife as thou wilt be, would make a man, after another campaign,—for another I must have, to satisfy the cravings of my appetite,—go nigh to forswear the wars.

MADELON
Ah, La Gloire! would it were so! but the sound of a trumpet will ever lead thee after it.

LA GLOIRE
Tut—a trumpet!—thy voice, Madelon, will drown it.

MADELON [Shaking her Head]
Ah, La Gloire!

LA GLOIRE
Nay, then, I am the veriest poltroon, if I think the sound of a trumpet would move me any more than—

[A Parley is sounded from the Walls.

—Eh!—gad—oh!—ecod there's a bustle! a parley from the walls; which may end in a skirmish, or a battle—or a—I'll be with you again in the chopping off of a head.

MADELON
Nay, now, La Gloire, I thought the sound of a trumpet—

LA GLOIRE
A trumpet—simpleton!—that was a—gad I—wasn't it a drum?—Adieu, Madelon! I'll be back again ere—

[Parley.

—March! —Charge!—Huzza!

[Draws his Sword, and exit.

MADELON

Well-a-day! a soldier's wife must have a fearful time on't. Yet do I love La Gloire; he is so kind, so tender!—and he has, simply, the best leg in the army. Heigho!—It must feel very odd to sleep in a tent:—a camp must be ever in alarms, and soldiers always ready for surprise.—Dame Toinette, who married a corporal, ere I was born, told me, that, for one whole campaign, her husband went to bed in his boots.

SONG.—MADELON.

Little thinks the townsman's wife,
While at home she tarries,
What must be the lass's life,
Who a soldier marries.
Now with weary marching spent,
Dancing now before the tent,
Lira, lira, lira, lira, lira la,
With her jolly soldier.
In the camp, at night, she lies,
Wind and weather scorning,
Only grieved her love must rise,
And quit her in the morning;
But the doubtful skirmish done,
Blithe she sings at set of sun;
Lira, lira, lira, lira, lira la,
With her jolly soldier.
Should the captain of her dear
Use his vain endeavour,
Whisp'ring nonsense in her ear,
Two fond hearts to sever,
At his passion she will scoff;
Laughing, thus, she'll put him off,—
Lira, lira, lira, lira, lira la,
For her jolly soldier.

[Exit.

SCENE II

The Town Hall of Calais

CITIZENS, **SOLDIERS**, and **CRIER**, discovered.

CRIER

Silence!—An ye all talk thus, there's an end to conversation. Your silence, my masters, will breed a disturbance. Mass, 'tis hard that I, who am Crier, should be laughed at, and held at nought among you.

ALL

Hear! hear!

CRIER
Listen.—The good John de Vienne, our governor—a blessing on his old merry heart!—grieving for your distress, has, e'en now, called a parley on the walls, with the English; and has chosen me, in his wisdom, to ring you all into the town hall, here; where, an you abide his coming, you will hear, what he shall seem to signify unto you. And, by our lady, here the governor comes!—

[Rings.

—Silence!

ALL
Silence!

CRIER
Nay, 'tis ever so. An I were to bid a dumb man hold his tongue, by my troth, I think a' would cry "Silence," till the drum of my ear were bursten. Silence!

[Enter **JOHN de VIENNE**, **EUSTACHE de St. PIERRE** following. **JOHN de VIENNE** seats himself at the Head of the Council Table; **EUSTACHE** sits in the Front, among the **CITIZENS**.

JOHN de VIENNE
You partly know why I have here convened you.
I pr'ythee, now,—I pr'ythee, honest friends!
Summon up all the fortitude within you,
Which you are masters of. Now, Heaven forgive me!
I almost wish I had not been a soldier;—
For I have, here, a matter to deliver
Requires a schoolman's preface. 'Tis a task,
Which bears so heavy on my poor old heart,
That 'twill go nigh to crack beneath the burden.
You know I love you, fellow citizens:
You know I love you well.

ALL
Ay, ay; we know it.

JOHN de VIENNE
I could be well content, in peace, or peril,
To 'bide with you for ever.

EUSTACHE
No one doubts it.
I never, yet, did hear of governor,
Spite of the rubs, and watchful toil of office,
Would willingly forego his place.

JOHN de VIENNE

Why, how now!
Why, how now, friend! dost thou come o'er me thus?
But I shall find a time—it fits not now—
When I will teach thee—'Sdeath! old John de Vienne,
A veteran, bluff soldier, bearded thus!
And sneer'd at by a saucy—Mark you me!—

[Rises.

Well, let it pass:—the general calamity
Will sour the best of us.—

[Sits.

—My honest citizens,
I once more pray you, think that ye are men:
I pray you, too, my friends—

EUSTACHE

I pray you, sir,
Be somewhat brief; you'll tire else. These same citizens
These honest citizens, would fain e'en know
The worst at once. When members are impatient
For a plain tale, the orator, (you'll pardon me,)
Should not be too long winded.

JOHN de VIENNE

Fellow, peace!
Ere now I've mark'd thee.—Thou art he, I take it,—
'Tis Eustache de St. Pierre, I think, they call thee—
Whom all the town, our very children, point at,
As the most growling knave in christendom;—
Yea, thou art he.

EUSTACHE

The same. The mongrels, here,
Cannot abide rough honesty:—I'm hated.
Smooth talking likes them better:—You, good sir,
Are popular among them.

ALL

Silence!

EUSTACHE

Buz!

JOHN de VIENNE

Thus, then, in brief. Finding we are reduced,
By famine, and fatigue, unto extremity,
I sounded for a parley from the walls;—
E'en now 't has ended:—Edward order'd forth
Sir Walter Manny; and I needs must own,
A courteous knight, although an enemy.—
I told him our distress. Sir Knight, said I—
And here it makes me almost blush to think
An Englishman should see me drop a tear;
But, 'spite of me, it stole upon my cheek;—
To speak the honest truth, Sir Knight, said I,
My gallant men are perishing with hunger:—
Therefore I will surrender.

EUSTACHE
Surrender!

[The rest look amazed.

JOHN de VIENNE
But, conceive me,
On this condition;—that I do secure
The lives, and liberties, of those brave fellows,
Who, in this galling and disastrous siege,
Have shared with me in each fatigue and peril.

ALL
Huzza! Long live our governor! Huzza!

JOHN de VIENNE
I thank you, friends.—It grieves me to repay
Your honest love, with tidings, sure, as heavy
As ever messenger was charged withal.
The King of England steels his heart against us.
He does let loose his vengeance; and he wills,—
If we would save our city from the sword,
From wild destruction,—that I straight do send him
Six of my first and best reputed citizens,
Bare headed, tendering the city keys;
And,—'sdeath, I choke!—with vile and loathsome ropes,
Circling their necks, in guise of malefactors,
To suffer instant execution.

[The **CITIZENS** appear confounded. A Pause.

Friends,
I do perceive you're troubled:—'tis enough
To pose the stoutest of you. Who among you

Can smother nature's workings, which do prompt
Each, to the last, to struggle for himself?
Yet, were I not objected to, as governor,
There might be found—no matter.—Who so bold,
That, for the welfare of a wretched multitude,
Involved with him, in one great common cause,
Would volunteer it on the scaffold?

EUSTACHE [Rises]
I:—
E'en I;—the growling knave, whom children point at.
To save those children, and their hapless mothers,
To snatch the virgin from the ravisher,
To shield the bent and hoary citizen,
To push the sword back from his aged throat,
(Fresh reeking, haply, in his house's blood,)
I render up myself for sacrifice.—
Will no one budge? Then let the English in;
Let in the enemy, to find us wasted,
And winking in the socket. Rouse, for shame!
Rouse, citizens! Think on your wives, your infants!
And let us not be so far shamed in story,
That we should lack six men within our walls,
To save them thus from slaughter.

JOHN de VIENNE
Noble soul!
I could, for this, fall down and worship thee.
Thou warm'st my heart. Does no one else appear,
To back this gallant veteran?
D'Aire. Eustache,—
Myself, and these two brothers, my companions,
All of your house, and near of kin to you,
Have ponder'd on your words:—we sure must die,
If we or go, or stay:—but, what weighs most—
We would not see our helpless little ones
Butcher'd before our eyes. We'll go with thee.

EUSTACHE
Now, by our good St. Dennis,
I do feel proud! My lowly house's glory
Shall live on record. What are birth and titles?
Feathers for children. The plain honest mind,
That branches forth in charity and virtue,
Shrinks lordly pomp to nought; and makes vain pedigree
Blush at his frothy boasting.—We are four;—
Fellows in death and honour.—Two remain
To fill our number.

JOHN de VIENNE [To **EUSTACHE**]
Pause a while, my friends;
We yet have breathing time;—though troth but little.—
I must go forth, a hostage to the English,
Till you appear. Break up our sad assembly;—
And, for the rest, agree among yourselves.
Were the time apt, I could well waste a year
In praising this your valour.

EUSTACHE
Break we up. If any
Can wind his sluggish courage to the pitch,
Meet me anon i'th' market-place: and, thence,
Will we march forth. Ye have but this, remember;
Either plunge bravely into death, or wait
Till the full tide of blood flows in upon you,
And shame and slaughter overwhelm us. Come;
My noble partners, come!

[Exeunt.

SCENE III

An apartment in the Governor's House

Enter **JULIA** and **RIBAUMONT**.

RIBAUMONT
Yet, hear me, Julia—

JULIA
Pr'ythee, good my lord,
Press me not thus: my father's strict command—
I must not say 'tis harsh—forbids me listen.

RIBAUMONT
Is then the path of duty so precise,
That 'twill not for a little deviate?
Sweet, let it wind, and bend to recollection.
Think on our oaths; yes, lady, they are mutual:—
You said you loved; I treasured the confession,
As misers hoard their gold: nay, 'twas my all.—
Think not I chatter in the idle school
Of whining coxcombs, where despair and death
Are words of course; I swell not fancied ills

With windy eloquence: no, trust me, Julia,
I speak in honest, simple suffering:
And disappointment, in my life's best hope,
So feeds upon my life, and wears me inward,
That I am nearly spirit-broken.

JULIA

Why, why this, my lord?
You urge me past a maiden's modesty.
What should I say?—In nature's course, my lord,
The parent sits at helm, in grey authority,
And pilots the child's action: for my father,
You know what humour sways him.

RIBAUMONT

Yes, court policy;
Time-serving zeal: tame, passive, blind, obedience
To the stern will of power; which doth differ
As wide from true, impulsive loyalty,
As puppet work from nature. O, I would
The time were come!—our enemy, the English,
Bid fairest first to show a bright example;
When, 'twixt the ruler and the ruled, affection
Shall be reciprocal: when majesty
Shall gather strength from mildness; and the subject
Shall look with duteous love upon his sovereign,
As the child eyes its father. Now, by Heaven!
Old John de Vienne is turn'd a temporiser;
Making his daughter the poor topmost round
Of his vile ladder to preferment. 'Sdeath!
And you to suffer this! O, fie, fie, Julia!
'Twould show more noble in you to lay bare
Your mind's inconstancy, than thus to keep
The semblance of a passion; meanly veiling
Your broken faith with the excuse of duty.
Out on't! 'tis shallow—you ne'er loved.

JULIA

My lord, my cup of sorrow was brimfull; and you,
I look'd not for it, have thrown in a drop,
Which makes it overflow. No more of that:
You have reviled my father: me, too, Ribaumont;
Heaven knows, I little merit it!—My lord,
Upon this theme we must not meet again.—
Farewell! and do not, do not think unkindly
On her, you, once, did call your Julia.
If it will sooth your anguish, Ribaumont,
To find a fellowship in grief, why think

That there is one, while struggling for her duty,
Sheds many a tear in private.—Heaven be with you!

[Exit.

RIBAUMONT
Stay, stay, and listen to me. Gone! and thus too!
And have I lost thee—and for ever, Julia?
Now do I look on life as the worn mariner,
Stretching his eyes o'er seas immeasurable,
And all is drear and comfortless. Henceforward,
My years will be one void; day roll on day,
In sameness infinite, without a hope
To chequer the sad prospect. O! if death
Came yoked with honour to me, I could, now,
Embrace it with as warm and willing rapture,
As mothers clasp their infants.

[Enter **LA GLOIRE**.

Now, La Gloire! what is the news?

LA GLOIRE
Good faith, my lord, the saddest that ever tongue told!

RIBAUMONT
What is't?

LA GLOIRE
The town has surrendered.

RIBAUMONT
I guessed as much.

LA GLOIRE
Upon conditions.

RIBAUMONT
What are they?

LA GLOIRE
Very scurvy ones, my lord.—To save the city from sacking, six citizens must swing for it, in Edward's camp. But four have yet been found; and they are—

RIBAUMONT
Who?

LA GLOIRE

Oh lord!—all of my own family.—There's John d'Aire, Jacque, and Pierre Wissant; my three good cousins german, my lord: and the fourth, who was the first that offered, is—is—

RIBAUMONT
Who, La Gloire?

LA GLOIRE [Wiping his Eyes]
I crave your pardon, my lord, for being thus unsoldier-like; but 'tis—'tis my own father.

RIBAUMONT
Eustache!

LA GLOIRE
He, my lord! He! old Eustache de St. Pierre:—the honestest, kindliest soul!—I cannot talk upon't.—Grief plays the hangman with me, and has almost choked me already.

RIBAUMONT
Why, I am courted to't.—The time, example,
Do woo me to my very wish.—Come hither.
Two, it should seem, are wanting, to complete
The little band of those brave men, who die
To save their fellows.

LA GLOIRE
Ay, my lord. There is a meeting upon't, half an hour hence, in the market-place.

RIBAUMONT
Mark me, La Gloire: and see, that you obey me,
Ev'n to the very letter of my orders.
They are the last, perhaps, my honest fellow,
I e'er shall give thee. Seek thy father out,
And tell him this from me: his gallant bearing
Doth school his betters; I have studied o'er
His noble lesson, and have learnt my duty.
Say, he will find me in the market-place,
Disguised in humble seeming; and I fain
Would pass for one allied to him: and thence—
Dost mark me well?—I will along with him,
Ev'n hand in hand, to death.

LA GLOIRE
My lord,—I—I—

[Bursts into tears, falls on his Knees, takes hold of **RIBAUMONT'S** Hand, and kisses it.

—I shall lose my father; when he was gone, I looked you would have been my father. The thought of still serving you was a comfort to me.—You are my commander; and I hope I have, hitherto, never disebeyed orders; but, if I now deliver your message, drum me out for ingratitude, as the greatest rascal that ever came into a regiment.

RIBAUMONT
Pr'ythee, no more, La Gloire? I am resolved;—
My purpose fix'd. It would be bitter to thee,
To see me die in anger with thee: therefore,
Do thou my bidding; close thy service up,
In duty to my will. Go, find thy father;
I will prepare within the while.—Obey me,—
Or the last look from thy expiring master,
Darting reproach, shall burst thy heart in twain.

Mark, and be punctual!

[Exit.

LA GLOIRE
O, the Virgin! Why was I ever attached to man, woman, or child?

[Enter **EUSTACHE de St. PIERRE**.

EUSTACHE
Where's thy commander, boy—Count Ribaumont?

LA GLOIRE
O father!—

EUSTACHE
Peace!—I must a word with him.
I have a few short thanks I would deliver,
Touching his care of thee: it is the last
Of all my worldly packages; that done,
I may set forward on my journey.

LA GLOIRE
Oh, father! I shall never go to bed again in peace as long as I live. Sorrow will keep my eyes open half the night; and when I drop into a doze at day-break, I shall be hanged with you, father, a score of times every morning.

EUSTACHE
I could have spared this meeting.—Boy, I will not—
Nor would I, had I time for't, ring a chime
Of drowsy document, at this, our parting.
Nor will I stuff the simple plan of life,
That I would have thee follow, with trim angles,
And petty intersections of nice conduct;
Which dotards, rotten in their wisdom, oft

Will mark, in mathematical precision,
Upon a stripling's mind, until they blur
The modest hand of nature. Thou'rt a soldier;
'Tis said a good one;—and I ne'er yet knew
A rough, true soldier, lack humanity:—
If, then, thou canst, with one hand, push aside
The buffets of the world, and, with the other,
Stretch'd forth, in warm and manly charity,
Assist the weak,—be thankful for the ground-work,
And e'en let impulse build upon't;—thou needst
No line, nor level, formal age can give thee,
To raise a noble superstructure. Come;
Embrace me;—when thy father sleeps in honour,
Think that—

[Embracing him, he bursts into Tears.

—my son, my boy!—Psha! pish! this nature—

Conduct me to—

LA GLOIRE [Catching hold of him]
Hold! hold!—We shall leap here, from bad to worse. I—I am bidden, father, to deliver a message to you.

EUSTACHE
Be quick, then; the time wears.

LA GLOIRE
No, truly, 'twill not come quick. I must force it out in driblets. My captain bids me say, that—that brave men are scarce. Find six in the town, and you find all;—so he will join you at the market-cross, and—go with you—to—

EUSTACHE
The scaffold!

LA GLOIRE
Yes, the sca—that word sticks so in my throat, I can't squeeze it out, for the life of me.

EUSTACHE
Why, this shows nobly now! our honest cause
Is graced in the addition. Lead me—

[Observing **LA GLOIRE**, weeping

—how now?
Out on thee, knave! thou'lt bring disgrace upon me.
By Heaven! I feel as proud in this, my death;—
And thou, the nearest to my blood, to sully

My house's name with womanhood—Shame! shame!
Where is the noble Ribaumont?

[Going.

LA GLOIRE
Stay, father, stay! I can hold it no longer. I love Madelon too well to keep her waking o'nights, with blubbering over her for the loss of my father, and my captain:—another neck is wanting to make up the half dozen; so I'll e'en along, father, as the sixth.

EUSTACHE [After a Pause]
I know not what to answer.—Thou hast shaken
My manhood to the centre.—Follow, boy!
Thy aim is honour; but the dreary road to't,
Which thou must tread, does stir the father in me.
'Tis such a nice and tickle point, between
The patriot and the parent, that, Heaven knows,
I need a counsellor.—I'll to thy captain.
With him, anon, you'll find me.

[Exit.

LA GLOIRE
So! how many a lad, with a fair beginning of life, comes to an untimely conclusion!—My poor Madelon, too! she little thinks that—

[**MADELON** peeping in.

MADELON
Hist! hist! La Gloire!

LA GLOIRE
Eh?

MADELON
Why, where hast thou been, La Gloire? I have been seeking you all over the town. I feared you would get into danger. Finding the Governor's gate thrown open, and all the city in confusion, I e'en ventured in to look for you. Where hast thou been, La Gloire?

LA GLOIRE
Been? no where—but I am going—

MADELON
Where, La Gloire?

LA GLOIRE
A—a little way with my father. Hast heard the news, Madelon?

MADELON

Only in part. I hear the town has surrendered: and that six poor men are to be executed; and march from the town gates. But we shall then be in safety, La Gloire. Poor fellows! I would not see them go forth for the world!

LA GLOIRE

Poor fellows!—a hem!—Ay, poor fellows! True, Madelon; I would not have thee shocked with the sight, I confess.

MADELON

But, pr'ythee, La Gloire, keep at home now with me. You are ever gadding. You soldiers are so wild and turbulent—How can you, La Gloire? You must be present, now, at this horrid ceremony?

LA GLOIRE

Why, truly, I—I must be present;—but it will be for the last time, Madelon. I take little pleasure, in it, believe me.

MADELON

I would thou wouldst home with me! I have provided, out of thy bounty, a repast for us this evening. My father, who has ne'er stirred out these three weeks, is filled with joy for thy return;—he will sit at our table, La Gloire; he will give us his blessing, and wish us happy in marriage. Come, you shall not away, this evening, in sooth, now!

LA GLOIRE

I must, Madelon; I must. The throng will press, and—and I may lose somewhat of value. 'Tis seldom a soldier's pocket is heavy; but I carry all my worldly goods about me. I would fain not lose it; so e'en be mistress on't till my return. Here is a casket;—with five years' wages from my captain; three quarters' pay from my regiment; and eleven marks, plucked from the boot of a dead English corporal: 'tis my whole fortune; keep it, Madelon, for fear of accidents: and if any cross accident ever should befall me, remember, you are heir apparent to the bulk of my property.

MADELON

But why thus particular? I would you would stay quiet with me!

LA GLOIRE

But for this once, Madelon; and I shall be quiet ever after.—Kiss me. So;—Adieu!

MADELON

Adieu, La Gloire! Remember, now, at night—

LA GLOIRE

Adieu!—At night!—Mercy on me!—should I stay three minutes longer, my heart would rescue my neck; for the breaking of one, would save the stretching of the other.

[Aside.—Exit.

MADELON

How rich my La Gloire has got in the wars! My father, too, has something to throw in at our wedding: and, when we meet, we shall be the happiest couple in Picardy.

SONG.—MADELON.
I tremble to think, that my soldier's so bold;
To see with what danger he gets all his gold;
Yet danger all over, 'twill keep out the cold,
And we shall be warm when we're married,
For riches, 'tis true that I covet them not,
Unless 'tis to better my dear soldier's lot;
And he shall be master of all I have got,
The very first moment we're married.
My heart how it beats, but to look to the day,
In church, when my father will give me away!
But that I shall laugh at, I've heard many say,
A day or two after we're married.

[Exit.

SCENE IV

Calais

A Gate, leading out of the Town.

Enter **CITIZENS**.

1ST CITIZEN
Stand back; they are coming.

3RD CITIZEN
Nay, my masters, they will not forth, this quarter of an hour. Men seldom move lightly on such a heavy occasion.

4TH CITIZEN
Who are the two others that have filled up the number?

3RD CITIZEN
Marry, two more of old Eustache's family. His own son; and the other, as 'tis rumoured, a relation, in the town, that few of us are acquainted withal.

4TH CITIZEN
That's strange.

3RD CITIZEN

Why, ay; but when a man chuses a rope for his preferment, few are found envious enough to dispute the title with him.—By the rood! here they come!

[Enter **EUSTACHE de St. PIERRE**, **RIBAUMONT**, **LA GLOIRE**, **JOHN D'AIRE**, **J. WISSANT**, **P. WISSANT**, going to execution: a Procession of **SOLDIERS**, **FRIARS**, **NUNS**, &c. accompanying them.—A solemn March; then, a Halt.

RIBAUMONT
I pr'ythee, peace, Eustache! I fain would 'scape
Observance from the rabble. Hurry o'er
This irksome march; and straightway to the camp.

EUSTACHE
Enough—Set forth! We are engaged, my friends,
Upon a business here, which most, I wot,
Do think of moment; and we would not waste
The time in idle ceremony. On!—
Ere we are usher'd to the English camp,
And most of you, I trust, will follow thither,—
We will bestow the little time allow'd us
In manly leave-ta**KING**
Strike, and set onward!

CITIZENS
Bless our countrymen! Bless our deliverers!

GLEE.—By the Persons of the Procession.
Peace to the heroes! peace! who yield their blood,
And perish, nobly, for their country's good!
Peace to their noble souls! their bodies die;
Their fame shall flourish long in memory;
Recorded still, in future years,
Green in a nation's gratitude, and tears.

CHORUS
Sound! sound in solemn strains, and slow!
Dully beat the muffled drum!
Bid the hollow trumpet blow,
In deaden'd tones, clear, firm, and low;—
For, see! the patriot heros come!

[Towards the End of the Chorus, the **CHARACTERS** proceed on their March out of the Town; and when the last **PERSONS** of the Procession are going through the Gates, the Curtain drops.

ACT THE THIRD

Enter **JULIA**, in Man's Apparel, and **O'CARROL**.

JULIA

Come on; bestir thee, good fellow! Thou must be my guide, and conduct me.

O'CARROL

'Faith, and I'll conduct you, with all my heart and soul; and some good creature, I warrant, will be kind enough to show me the way.

JULIA

But art thou well assured, O'Carrol, of what thou hast informed me?

O'CARROL

To be sure I am well assured; for I informed myself, and I never yet catched myself out in telling a lie. There was six of them, as tall fellows as any in France, with ugly ropes about their good-looking necks, going to the town-gates; and Count Ribaumont marched second in the handsome half dozen. The whole town followed them with their eyes, till they were as full of water as if they had been peeping into so many mustard pots. And so, madam, knowing he loves you better than dear life,(which, to be sure, he seems to hold cheap enough at present), and thinking you would be glad to hear the terrible news, why, I made all the haste I could to come and tell it to you.

JULIA

And thus, in haste, have I equipped myself. Come, good O'Carrol;—dost think I shall 'scape discovery in these accoutrements?

O'CARROL

Escape!—By my soul, lady, one would think you had been a young man, from the very first day you were born. Och! what a piece of work a little trimming and drapery makes in a good fellow's fancy! A foot is a foot, all the world over;—but take the foot of the sweetest little creature that ever tripped over green sward, and if it doesn't play at bo-peep under a petticoat—'faith, I don't know the reason of it; but it gives a clean contrary turn to a man's imagination. But what is it you would be after now, Lady Julia?

JULIA

Something I will do; and it must be speedy: at all hazards, we will to the English camp, O'Carrol:— opportunity must shape the rest.

O'CARROL

The camp?—O, 'faith, that's my element; and Heaven send us success in it! If an Irishman's prayers, lady, could make you happy, your little heart should soon be as light as a feather-bed.

JULIA

I thank thee, my honest fellow: thy care for me shall not long go unrewarded.

O'CARROL

Now the devil fetch rewarding, say I! If a man does his best friends a piece of service, he must be an unconscionable sort of an honest fellow, to look for more reward than the pleasure he gets in assisting them.

JULIA
Well, well! each moment now is precious! Haste thee, O'Carrol; Time has wings.

O'CARROL
Och! be asey, madam; we'll take the ould fellow by the forelock, I warrant him. When honest gentlemen's business calls them on a small walk to the gallows, a man may set out a quarter of an hour behind them, and be certain of meeting them upon the road:—and, now I bethink me, madam, if we go out at the draw-bridge, from the citadel, hard by the house here, we may be at the camp, ere the poor souls have marched their body round the battlements.

JULIA
Thou say'st well; and we will forth that way:

'Twill be most private too. Thou'lt follow me, O'Carrol?

O'CARROL
Ay, that I would, to the end of the wide world, and a thousand miles beyond it.

JULIA
Yet, tarry here a while, till I prepare the means of our going forth.
Join me a few minutes hence in the hall, O'Carrol.
And, Fortune, frown not on a poor weak woman!
Who, if she fail in this, her last, sad struggle,
Is so surrounded by a sea of grief
That she must sink for ever!

[Exit.

O'CARROL
And, sink or swim, I'll to the bottom along with you.—Och! what a sad thing it is to see sorrow wet the sweet cheeks of a woman! Faith, now, I can't make out that same crying, for the life of me. My sorrow is always of a dry sort; that gives me a sore throat, without ever-troubling my eyes about the business. The camp! Well, with all my heart: it won't be the first time I have been present at a bit of a bustle.

SONG.—O'CARROL.
When I was at home, I was merry and frisky;
My dad kept a pig, and my mother sold whisky:
My uncle was rich, but would never be asy,
Till I was enlisted by Corporal Casey.
Oh! rub a dub, row de dow, Corporal Casey!
My dear little Sheelah I thought would run crazy,
When I trudged away with tough Corporal Casey.
I march'd from Kilkenny, and as I was thinking
On Sheelah, my heart in my bosom was sinking;

But soon I was forced to look fresh as a daisy,
For fear of a drubbing from Corporal Casey.
Och! rub a dub, row de dow, Corporal Casey!
The devil go with him, I ne'er could be lazy,
He stuck in my skirts so, ould Corporal Casey.
We went into battle; I took the blows fairly,
That fell on my pate, but they bother'd me rarely:
And who should the first be that dropp'd? why, an plase ye,
It was my good friend, honest Corporal Casey.
Och! rub a dub, row de dow, Corporal Casey!
Thinks I, you are quiet, and I shall be asy;
So eight years I fought, without Corporal Casey.

[Exit.

SCENE II

The English Camp

A Scaffold in the Back of the Scene: **TWO WORKMEN** descend from it.

1ST WORKMAN
There 'tis;—and finished: as pleasing a piece of work, as man could wish to turn out of hand. If King Edward, (Heaven bless him!) give me not a pension for this, let'n make the next scaffold himself. Mass! I would (with reverence be it spoken), build a scaffold, and fix a gallows, with any king in Christendom.

2ND WORKMAN
Yea, marry, if he had not served his time to the trade.

1ST WORKMAN
Yea, or if he had. I have been prime gallows maker, and principal hangman, now, nine-and-twenty years.—Thank Heaven! neighbour, I have long been notorious.

2ND WORKMAN
Thou say'st true, indeed. Thy enemies cannot deny thee that.

1ST WORKMAN
And why, I pray you? why have I been so?

2ND WORKMAN
Mass, I know not! I think 'tis thy good luck.

1ST WORKMAN
Tut, I will tell thee. My parents, I thank them, bred me to the gallows: marry, then, how was it?—why, look you, I took delight in my business.—An you would be a good workman, ever, while you live, take a

delight in your business. I have been an honest, pains-taking man, neighbour. No one is notorious, without taking pains for it.

2ND WORKMAN
Truly, then, I fear my character is naught. I never can bring myself to take pains for it.

1ST WORKMAN
Thou art the more to be pitied. I never made but one small mistake, since I entered on business.

2ND WORKMAN
I pr'ythee, now, tell me that.

1ST WORKMAN
'Twas on execution day; we were much thronged, and the signal was given full soon; when, a pize on it! I whips me, in haste, the halter over the neck of an honest stander-by:—and I jerks me him up to the top of a twenty foot gibbet. Marry, the true rogue escaped by't; for 'twas a full hour ere the error was noted. But, hast heard who the six be, that will be here anon?

2ND WORKMAN
Only that they be citizens. They are e'en now coming hitherward. Some of our men have seen them: they march, as 'tis reported, wondrous doleful.

1ST WORKMAN
No matter; tarry till they see my work;—that's all. An that do not content them, mark them for sour knaves. An a man be not satisfied when a sets foot on my scaffold, say he is hard to please. Rot them, your condemned men, now-a-days, have no discernment. I would I had the hanging of all my fellow craft! I should then have some judges of my skill; and merit would not go praiseless.—

[A Flourish.

—So!—the king is coming—stand clear, now, neighbour:—an the king like not my scaffold, I am no true man.

[They go on the Scaffold.

[Enter **KING EDWARD, QUEEN PHILIPPA, HARCOURT, SIR WALTER MANNY, ARUNDEL, WARWICK, TRAIN-BEARERS, STANDARDS,** &c.

KING
Yes, good Philippa, 'tis our firm decree,
And a full wise one too;—'tis but just recompense,
For near twelve weary months, their stubbornness
Has caused us linger out before their city.
Should we not now resent, in future story
Our English would be chronicled as dullards;—
These French would mock us for the snails of war,
Who bring our houses on our sluggish backs,
To winter it before their mould'ring walls;

Nay, every village, circled by a ditch,
Would think itself a town impregnable;
Check the full vigour of our march, and worry
Our armies with resistance.

QUEEN PHILIPPA
And yet, my liege, I cannot chuse but pity
The wretched men, who now must suffer for it.

KING
Justice, madam,
Minute in her stern exercise of office,
Is comprehensive in effect; and when
She points her sword to the particular,
She aims at general good.—

[Solemn Music, at a Distance.

But, hark! they come.
Are they within our lines?

SIR WALTER MANNY
They are, my liege.

KING
Deliver up Sir John de Vienne.

[**KING EDWARD** and **QUEEN PHILIPPA** seat themselves on a Throne, erected in the Camp, on the
occasion of the Execution.

[Enter **EUSTACHE de St. PIERRE**, with the Keys; **RIBAUMONT, LA GLOIRE, JOHN d'AIRE, J. WISSANT**, and
P. WISSANT, with Halters round their Necks; a Multitude of **FRENCH** following.

KING
Are these the six must suffer?

EUSTACHE
Suffer!—no:—
We do embrace our fate: we glory in't.
They who stand forward, sir, to yield their lives,
A willing forfeit, for their country's safety,
When they meet death, meet honour, and rejoice
In the encounter. Suffer, is a term
The upright, and undaunted spirit, blots
From death's vocabulary.

KING
Now, beshrew thee, knave!

Thou dost speak bluntly.

EUSTACHE
Ay, and cheerily.
But to our purpose.—I am bidden, sir,
I and my noble comrades, here, of Calais,
Thus lowly, at your feet, to tender to you
Our city's keys;—

[Kneels and lays the Keys at the Foot of the Throne.

—and they do guard a treasure

Well worth a king's acceptance; for they yield
A golden opportunity to mightiness
Of comforting the wretched. Take but these,
And turn our ponderous portals on the hinge,
And you will find, in every street, a document,
A lesson, at each step, for iron power
To feel for fellow men:—Our wasted soldiers
Dropping upon their watch; the dying mother
Wailing her famish'd child; the meagre son
Grasping his father's hand in agony,
Till their sunk eyes exchange a feeble gleam
Of love and blessing, and they both expire.

KING
Your citizens may thank themselves for't; wilfulness
Does ever thus recoil upon itself.

EUSTACHE
Sworn liegemen to their master, and their monarch,
They have perform'd their duty, sir. I trust
You, who yourself are king, can scarcely blame
Poor fellows for their loyalty. 'Tis plain
You do not, sir; for now, your royal nature
O'erflows in clemency; and setting by
All thought of crushing those beneath your feet,
Which, in the heat and giddiness of conquest,
The victor sometimes is seen guilty of;
Our town finds grace and pity at your hands.
Your noble bounty, sir, is pleas'd consider
Some certain trifles we have suffer'd; such
As a bare twelvemonth's siege—a lack of food;
Some foolish grey-beards dead by't; some few heaps
Of perish'd soldiers; and, humanely weighing
These nothings as misfortunes, spare our people:
Simply exacting, that six useless citizens,

Mere logs in the community, and prized
For nothing but their honesty, come forth,
Like malefactors, and be gibbetted!

KING
Villain and slave! for this thy daring taunt,
(Howe'er before we might incline to listen),
We henceforth shut the ear to supplication.

EUSTACHE
Mighty sir!
We march'd not forth to supplicate, but die.
Trust me, king,
We could not covet aught, in your disposal,
Would swell our future name with half the glory
As this same sentence, which, we thank you for't,
You have bestow'd, unask'd.

KING
Conduct them straight to execution!

LA GLOIRE [Advancing to the left of **EUSTACHE**]
Father!

EUSTACHE
How now? thou shakest!

LA GLOIRE
'Tisn't for myself, then.—For my own part, I am a man: but I cannot look on our relations, and my captain, and on you, father, without feeling a something, that makes a woman of me.—But I—

EUSTACHE
Briefly, boy; what is't?

LA GLOIRE
Give me thy hand, father! So—

[Kisses it.

—And now, if I part with it, while a puff of breath remains in my body, I shall lose one of the most sorrowful comforts, that ever poor fellow in jeopardy fixed his heart upon. Were I but well assured poor Madelon would recover the news, I could go off as tough as the stoutest.

RIBAUMONT [Advances to the right of **EUSTACHE**]
Farewell, old heart! thy body doth incase
The noblest spirit soldier e'er could boast,
To face grim death withal. Inform our fellows,
At the last moment given, on the scaffold,

We will embrace, and—

[A Muffled Drum beats.

—Hark! the signal beats.

EUSTACHE
Lead on.

[They march up to the Scaffold.

SOLDIER [Without]
You cannot pass.

JULIA [Without]
Nay, give me way!

[Enter **JULIA** and **O'CARROL**.

JULIA
Stay, stay your hands! desist, or—

KING
How now!
Wherefore this boldness?

JULIA
Great and mighty King!
Behold a youth much wrong'd. Men do esteem
The Monarch's throne as the pure fount and spring
Whence justice flows: and here I cry for it.

KING
What is the suit thus urges?

JULIA
Please you, sir,
Suspend a while this fatal ceremony,—
For therein lies my grief,—and I will on.

KING
Pause ye a while.—Young man, proceed.

JULIA
Now, Heaven!
Make firm my woman's heart!
[Aside]
—Most royal sir!

Although the cause of this my suit doth wound
My private bosom, yet it doth involve,
And couple with me, a right noble sharer.—
'Tis you, great sir, you are yourself abused;
My countrymen do palter with thee, King:—
You did require
Six of our citizens, first in repute,
And best consider'd of our town, as victims
Of your high-throned anger. Here is one

[Pointing to **RIBAUMONT**.

I single out, and challenge to the proof;—
Let him stand forth;—and here I do avouch
He is no member of our city:
He does usurp another's right; defeats
Your mighty purpose: and your rage, which thirsted
For a rich draught of vengeance, must be served
With the mere dregs of our community.

RIBAUMONT [Advances]
Shame! I shall burst!—the dregs!—

KING
Thou self-will'd fool,
Who would run headlong into death, what art thou?

RIBAUMONT
A man:—let that content you, sir!—'Tis blood
You crave,—and with an appetite so keen,
'Tis strange to find you nice about its quality.
But for this slave,
Who thus has dared belie me, did not circumstance
Rein in my wish—(O grant me patience, Heaven!
The dregs!)—now, by my soul! I'd crush the reptile
Beneath my feet; now, while his poisonous tongue
Is darting forth its venom'd slander on me.

KING
I will be satisfied in this. Speak, fellow?
Say, what is thy condition?

RIBAUMONT
Truly, sir,
'Tis waste of royal breath to make this stir,
For one, whom some few minutes hence your sentence
Must sink to nothing. Henceforth I am dumb
To all interrogation.

KING
Now, by our diadem!—but answer you.
What is his state?—Say, of whose wreched place
Is he the bold usurper?

JULIA
Sir, of mine.
He does despoil me of my title; comes
Bedeck'd in my just dues; which, as a citizen,
(A young one though I be,) I here lay claim to.
I am your victim, sir; dismiss this man,
Who, haply, comes, in pity to my youth,
And plucks the glory from me, which this ceremony
Would grace my name withal, and let me die.

O'CARROL [Aside]
Die!—Och, the devil! did I come to the camp for this?—Madam, dear, dear madam!—

KING
The glory!—Why, by Heaven! these headstrong French
Toy with our punishments!
For thee, rash stripling! who dost brave our vengeance,
Prepare to meet it. Yoke thee with this knave,
Whose insolence hath roused our spleen, and, straight,
You both shall suffer for't together.

JULIA [Kneeling]
Sir!
Ere I do meet my fate, upon my knees
I make one poor request. This man, great sir!
(Tho' now, there's reason why he knows me not,)
I own doth touch me nearly.—I do owe him
A debt of gratitude;—'twould shock me sore
To see him in his agony;—so please you,
Command, that, in the order of our deaths,
I may precede him.

KING
Well;—so be it, then.—
Guards! lead them forth.

JULIA
And might he—oh, dread sir!
Might he but live, I then should be at peace.

KING
Conduct them to their fate.

JULIA [Rises]
Then, ere we go, a word at parting;—
For here your spleen o'erleaps the bound of prudence.
The blood you now would spill, is pure and noble;
Nor will the shedding of it lack avengers.
Shame on disguise! off with't, my lord!
[To **RIBAUMONT**]
—Behold
Our France's foremost champion: and remember,
In many a hardy fight, the gallant deeds
(For fame has blown them loudly King!) of Ribaumont.
Oft has he put you to't:—nay, late, at Cressy,
Ask of your Black Prince Edward, there, how long
Count Ribaumont and he were point to point.
He has attack'd our foe; reliev'd our people;
Succour'd our town, till cruel disappointment,
Where he had fix'd his gallant heart, did turn him
Wild with despairing love. Old John de Vienne
Denied his daughter to him;—drove him hither,
To meet your cruelty;—and now, that daughter,
Grown desperate as he, doth brave it, King!
And we will die together.

[Runs and embraces **RIBAUMONT**.

RIBAUMONT
Heaven!—my Julia!
Art thou then true?—O give me utterance!
Now, fortune, do thy worst!—

[Throws off his Disguise.

You cannot, King!
You dare not, for your life, lay savage hands
On female innocence!—and, for myself,
E'en use your will.

[**KING** descends from the Throne; **HARCOURT** kneels and offers his Arm; and the **QUEEN** descends, and goes opposite to the **KING**.

KING
Lady, you are free:—
Our British Knights are famed for courtesy;
And it will ne'er, I trust, be said an Englishman
Denied protection to a woman. You
Must, under guard, my lord! abide our pleasure:—
For the remainder, they have heard our will,

And they must suffer: 'tis but fit we prove,
Spite of their obstinate and close defence,
Our English excellence.

QUEEN PHILIPPA [Kneels]
Oh! then, my liege,
Prove it in mercy.
War, noble sir! when too far push'd, is butchery:
When manly victory o'erleaps its limits,
The tyrant blasts the laurels of the conqueror.
Let it not dwell within your thoughts, my liege,
Thus to oppress these men. And, royal sir!
Since you were free to promise
Whatever boon I begg'd,—now, on my knee,
I beg it, sir. Release these wretched men:
Make me the means of cheering the unhappy:
And, though my claim were tenfold what it is
Upon your bounty, 'twould reward me nobly.

KING
Rise, madam. Tho' it was our fix'd intent
To awe these French, by terrible example,
Our promise still is sacred, good Philippa.
Your suit is won; and we relax our rigour.—
Let them pass free; while we do here pronounce
A general pardon.

LA GLOIRE
A pardon! no!—Oh diable!—My father! and my commander too!—Huzza!—

[Takes the Rope from his Father's Neck, then from his own, and runs down with the **THREE KINSMEN**.

—Oh! that I should live to unrope my poor old father, and master!

[Runs to **RIBAUMONT**, and takes the Rope off his Neck.

[Enter **MADELON**.

[She and **LA GLOIRE** rush into each other's Arms.

MADELON
Oh! my poor La Gloire!—My tears—

LA GLOIRE
That's right! Cry, Madelon!—cry for joy, wench!—Old Eustache is safe!—my Captain and relations free!—Here's a whole bundle of honest necks recovered: mine's tossed in, in the lump; and we'll be married, Madelon, to-morrow.

KING [To **RIBAUMONT**]
Now, my lord! for you:—
We have, I trust, some influence here;
Nor will we quit your town, until we see
Your marriage solemnized—

O'CARROL
Well, if I didn't know what crying was before, I have found it out at last.—'Faith it has a mighty pleasant
relieving sort of a feel with it.

KING
Prepare we, then, to enter Calais; straight
Give order for our march—
Breathe forth, our instruments of war; and, as
We do approach the rugged walls, sound high
The strains of victory.

GRAND CHORUS.
Rear, rear our English banner high
In token proud of victory!
Where'er our god of battle strides,
Loud sound the trump of fame!
Where'er the English warrior rides,
May laurel'd conquest grace his name.

[Exeunt **OMNES**.

George Colman the Younger – A Concise Bibliography

The Female Dramatist (1782)
Two to One (1784)
Turk and No Turk (1785)
Inkle and Yarico (1787)
Ways and Means (1788)
The Battle of Hexham (1793)
The Iron Chest (1796)
The Heir at Law (1797)
The Poor Gentleman (1802)
John Bull, or an Englishman's Fireside (1803)

Colman was also the author of a great deal of so-called humorous poetry (usually coarse, though
popular) – My Night Gown and Slippers (1797), reprinted under the name of Broad Grins, in 1802; and
Poetical Vagaries (1812). Some of his writings were published under the assumed name of Arthur
Griffinhood of Turnham Green.

www.ingramcontent.com/pod-product-compliance
Lightning Source LLC
Chambersburg PA
CBHW021943040426
42448CB00008B/1215